Lemonade
Lessons
for Life

Refreshing Reminders
for Happier Living

❦

BRET NICHOLAUS
National Best-Selling Author of *THE CONVERSATION PIECE* Series

Warm Words Press
a division of William Randall Publishing
P.O. Box 340, Yankton, SD 57078
www.william-randall-publishing.com

Cover and text design by Mary Ann Hoebelheinrich • Yankton, SD
Design revisions by Ann Lundstrom • Elk Point, SD

Edited by Aldo Mungai • Western Springs, IL

William Randall Publishing's authors are available for seminars and speaking engagements.
If interested please contact us at the address listed above.

ATTENTION: SCHOOLS AND BUSINESSES
William Randall Publishing's books are available at quantity discounts
with bulk purchase for educational, business, or promotional use.
For more information, contact:
William Randall Publishing, Special Sales Department,
P.O. Box 340, Yankton, South Dakota 57078

ISBN #0-9755801-4-0

Printed in the United States of America

First Edition: March 2003
Second Edition: March 2005

10 9 8 7 6 5 4 3 2 1

∽

To my wife, my son, and my mom.
I love you all more than any words could ever express!

...and in very loving memory of my dad

JOHN 1:1-18

∽

Servings

LEMONADE LESSON ONE
People don't fail, they quit
4

LEMONADE LESSON TWO
*On life's highway, spend more time
in the right-hand lane*
12

LEMONADE LESSON THREE
Be a lighthouse, not an outhouse
18

LEMONADE LESSON FOUR
When you're feeling down, do like Duke
24

LEMONADE LESSON FIVE
*Silence is golden,
so make your words platinum*
28

LEMONADE LESSON SIX
Climb up, but reach down
34

LEMONADE LESSON SEVEN
*Make yourself rich by
making your wants few*
40

LEMONADE LESSON EIGHT
*Accept your limitations
and you'll expand your potential*
46

LEMONADE LESSON NINE
*Their interests, shared interests,
your interests—in that order*
52

LEMONADE LESSON TEN
*The happiness of your life depends
upon the quality of your thoughts*
60

LEMONADE LESSON ELEVEN
In all things, humility
66

LEMONADE LESSON TWELVE
*One person with passion
is better than forty who
are merely interested*
74

LEMONADE LESSON THIRTEEN
Remember Jack and Ben
82

LEMONADE LESSON FOURTEEN
*Be caring and compassionate—
constantly*
88

LEMONADE LESSON FIFTEEN
*Winning the rat race is
the ultimate trap*
94

LEMONADE LESSON SIXTEEN
Please, say "Thank you"
98

LEMONADE LESSON SEVENTEEN
*Accomplishments are
seldom bigger than
the size of your dreams*
104

LEMONADE LESSON EIGHTEEN
There are always more lessons to learn
112

It is not living that is important,
but living rightly.

—Socrates

Introduction

$\mathcal{W}$elcome to *Lemonade Lessons for Life*, a book that just might make you feel as good about life today as an ice-cold lemonade did on a hot summer afternoon when you were a child. If you like to be inspired and motivated, you've come to the right book!

What you are holding is a collection of 18 life-enhancing and potentially life-changing "lessons"—mainly original sayings, though occasionally I have chosen for the heading a famous quotation that says it far better than I ever could. Each lesson is followed by a series of short stories (sometimes taken from my personal experiences), examples, and quotations to help you apply that particular lesson to your own life. And much like a real glass of lemonade goes down quickly and easily, these "servings" were written in a way that can be read quickly and understood with ease—something you'll appreciate when you have only a few minutes to spare.

You'll discover that certain lessons are best applied to your personal or family life, while some are meant to be put to use in your career or on the job; others are intended simply to give you a positive jolt whenever you need it most. Some lessons are here to help you in your day-to-day activities and pursuits, while others will give you encouragement for the "big picture" throughout your lifetime. The lessons contained herein are for everyone, regardless of who you are, what you do, or where you are in your life right now. Since there is no particular order to the chapters, you can flip to any given chapter at any time and just start reading.

I strongly believe in each lesson I have chosen and do all

that I can to employ each one on a regular basis in my own life. A number of these lessons were taught to me when I was a child, but they ring just as true—if not more so—today. I'm sure that a fair share of the lessons contained in this book will serve as welcomed reminders of things *you* probably learned or were told at an earlier point in your life but may have since forgotten. Some of the lessons may touch on topics with which you are familiar, but they will give you a whole new perspective to consider. And of course, a few of the lessons will likely revolve around things that you have never thought about—until now. Regardless of whether the lessons are new or old to you, it is my sincere hope that each one will in some way refresh your soul and re-energize you like never before for life itself.

Enjoy!

—Bret Nicholaus

People Don't Fail, They Quit

We all know from personal experience that life is the great teacher of lessons. It seems as though every day another valuable lesson presents itself, whether at work, at leisure, or in the general day-to-day responsibilities that come with being an adult or having a family. But if you look back into your own days as a young child, you'll probably discover that you were learning the lessons of a lifetime even then...lessons that not only helped you at that particular moment or point in your life, but still help you even today. I'll never forget how, as an eight-year-old boy, I learned one of those lessons—one that most literally can be called a "lemonade lesson for life."

On a typically hot and humid Chicago afternoon in July, some neighborhood kids and I had decided to engage in a little business venture—selling lemonade from a stand at the end of my parents' driveway. It certainly seemed like the type of day on which there would be a strong demand for great-tasting, ice-cold lemonade; but for whatever reason people weren't stopping to buy. Of course as kids, patience was in short supply, and after an hour or so my "colleagues" began to abandon the business. "I guess this was a dumb idea after all," one kid huffed before he walked away from the stand. One by one they left, until I was the only one remaining out by the curb.

Undeterred, I decided to stand my ground and stick around. Another twenty or so minutes passed with no takers. Then another seemingly lengthy span of time with nothing to show for it. Then another. But ahhhhhhh, at about 3:00

or so, something wonderful and unanticipated happened—the neighborhood mailman walked up to the stand and asked if I would pour him a lemonade. After hauling around a heavy sack for the better part of a sweltering day, this customer was good and ready to have a cold drink poured for him. Within the minute, I distinctly remember his asking for another glass. Thirds? No problem! Three lemonades at 10 cents each came out to 30 cents, but this good-hearted gentleman dropped a dollar in the jar and told me to keep the change (to an eight-year-old in 1978, that was big-time cash!). While our neighborhood mailman was standing there enjoying his refreshment, some bike riders decided to stop. Then a lady pulled up in her car; she, too, wanted a drink. And once there were a few people standing around, a couple of neighbors decided to venture out of their homes to see what I had to offer. In addition to the mailman, other people also gave me extra change as a tip. By the time everyone had left, I had cleared better than $3.00—more than enough money to buy myself that new toy I had been wanting, and certainly enough money to have made all my extra effort worthwhile.

I suspect that about the time all those people were arriving at my stand and I was beginning to collect some cash, the three other kids were back home sulking, telling their moms how the lemonade idea had been a flop, a waste of time, a failure. As has often been the case for me since that first lemonade stand, fortitude and perseverance eventually won the day. Though the challenges of life and business are far more complex now than they were back then, the lesson remains exactly the same. In fact, as I work as both a writer and publisher in the extremely competitive book-publishing industry, the lesson I learned on that hot summer afternoon is even more applicable for me today. If you look closely and honestly at your own life or the lives of other individuals you know, I think you'll see that this lemonade lesson proves itself true time and time again:

People don't fail, they quit!

Consider the following two quotes from Thomas Edison, a man who had 1,093 patents in his own name alone—more than any other American in history.

*If I find 10,000 ways something won't work,
I haven't failed. I am not discouraged, because
every wrong attempt discarded is another step forward.
Just because something doesn't do what you planned it
to do doesn't mean it's useless.*

*Our greatest weakness lies in giving up.
The most certain way to succeed
is always to try one more time.*

American novelist Jack London received 600 rejection notices from publishers before he sold his first book. (Yes, you read that number correctly—600.) Talk about being willing to try one more time!

> *It is my belief that talent is truly plentiful,*
> *and that what is lacking is staying power.*
>
> —DORIS LESSING

Johannes Brahms, the famous 19th-century German composer who eventually wrote masterpieces in almost every form except opera, worked painstakingly for nearly 10 years to complete his first symphony. Brahms would say of composing, "It does not just come to you. It is torture."

*No one would have crossed the ocean
if he could have gotten off the ship in the storm.*

—Charles F. Kettering

*Nothing in the world can take the place of
persistence. Talent will not; nothing is more common
than unsuccessful people with talent. Genius will not;
unrewarded genius is almost a proverb. Education
will not; the world is full of educated failures.
Persistence and determination alone
are omnipotent.*

—Calvin Coolidge

*Perseverance is a great element of success.
If you only knock long enough and loud enough
at the gate, you are sure to wake up somebody.*

—Henry Wadsworth Longfellow

On Life's Highway, Spend More Time in the Right-Hand Lane

A few months ago, I was riding in the car with someone who was doing about 75 in a 55 m.p.h. zone. As he zipped past the slower cars in the right-hand lane, he scoffed, "What is it with these people that barely drive the speed limit and spend their time gazing out the window? It's not like there's anything worth seeing out there." Without realizing it, he had perfectly summarized how many people feel about life itself—people who are so busy trying to get to the next episode in their life that they fail to appreciate, or even see, the beauty of the moment they are in.

The late, famous Norwegian Thor Heyerdahl said a mouthful when he stated, "Progress is our ability to complicate simplicity." Due to all the modern-day technological advances and "conveniences" we have, the simple ways and pleasures of yesteryear seem to be vanishing for good. While our quality of life is supposedly the best it has ever been, we have less and less time to actually enjoy our lives. And the information highway moves us along at such breakneck speed that what we think of as new and ground-breaking today may very well be obsolete tomorrow.

Consider, for a moment, these words by James Truslow Adams:

Perhaps it would be a good idea, fantastic as it sounds, to muffle every telephone, stop every motor and halt all activity for one hour some day just to

*give people a chance to ponder what it is all about,
why they are living and what they really want.*

What do *you* want? What do you *really* want? More than
likely, happiness is at or very near the top of your list. If it is,
you are in very good company. More than 225 years ago, our
founding fathers thought the pursuit of happiness so incredibly important that they wrote it down in the *Declaration of
Independence* as one of our inalienable rights. The problem is,
most of us are so busy hurrying to the next point or stage in
our life—*pursuing* happiness—that we have very little time
to actually *be* happy. For many of us, happiness is always
around the next bend; but when we get around that bend, we
see yet another curve...around which—we think—happiness
must surely be waiting.

If you want to experience real happiness in our world, you
must learn to live in *this* moment—not tomorrow's
moments, or next week's, or next year's. Let's face it: None of

us knows if we are right now living in our final hours or days of this life. Do you really want to spend them rushing to get somewhere else, hurrying to get to another mountaintop experience down the road? Stop...and take time for today. Saturate yourself in the time you've been given right here, right now. You can never, ever get back the uniqueness of this particular point in time, so do whatever you can to savor this moment to its fullest potential.

On several occasions over the years I've come across the anonymous quote listed on the next page; since it's a popular quote, it's very possible that you've seen it, too. It's worth re-reading often, as it clearly reminds us that we had better enjoy each and every aspect of life's ride...lest we find that the trip is suddenly and unexpectedly over and we have missed so many wonderful sights along the way.

*First I was dying to finish high school
and start college. And then I was dying to
finish college and start working.
And then I was dying to marry and
have children. And then I was dying for my children
to grow old enough so I could go back to work.
And then I was dying to retire.
And now I am dying...
and suddenly realize that I forgot to live.*

—Source unknown

*On life's highway, spend more time
in the right-hand lane.*

Be a Lighthouse, Not an Outhouse

Whenever she has the opportunity to do so on vacation, my mom enjoys taking tours of famous lighthouses. In addition to visiting these lighthouses, she enjoys collecting miniature ones, as do several other people I know. In fact, not only do these individuals proudly collect miniature replicas of lighthouses, but just about everything else that features lighthouses: plates, decorative pillows, blankets, napkin holders, lamps with lighthouse finials, stationery with sketches of lighthouses...the list seems endless. Having walked through my fair share of art galleries over the years, I have to admit that some of the most beautiful paintings I've ever seen are seascapes that prominently incorporate lighthouses into the theme. I've been in retail stores that dedicated entire sections to lighthouse merchandise, so you know this lighthouse thing is serious business.

Having said that, let me go back to my mom for a second and say that she has never yet made it a point to visit a famous outhouse (is there such a thing?), nor does she collect miniature ones. Nobody else I know collects outhouse merchandise, either. They own no plates featuring outhouses, and no decorative pillows with them. No blankets, no stationery, no nothing with outhouses. Have you ever seen a breathtaking painting that features an outhouse? Have you ever walked into a store and found that they have apportioned several shelves of merchandise to outhouse-related products? The odds are strongly against it. People don't collect outhouse paraphernalia. People don't like to talk about outhouses. They are, quite frankly, a major turn-off—and in many ways the symbolic opposite of a lighthouse.

Metaphorically speaking, what are you—a lighthouse or an outhouse? Think for a moment of what a lighthouse really is or represents: A comfort that seafarers know they can count on to help them avoid dangerous shallows and shoals, a rock-solid tower, an ever-present light in the darkness, a strong beacon of hope. A lighthouse stands for all things good. An outhouse, on the other hand, has its own unique list of "features" that you no doubt could create with ease, but you would probably rather not. (Certainly the list would be filled with many negative words like *dark, decaying, dingy, dull, miserably hot* or *cold, reeking, rotten* and *suffocating*.)

The vast majority of people would of course be very quick to say that they are lighthouses...but are they really? Look very carefully one more time at what each "house" represents, and be completely honest with yourself. Are you someone that people are drawn to, or are you the type of person that other people would just as soon avoid if possible? What about such things as your character, your relationships, your spiritual life—are they pretty solid or are they in need of some serious repair? Are you making the world a *better* place or are you making it a *bitter* place?

The late Hindu leader and social reformer Mahatma Gandhi said, "My life is my message." Does your message shine or stink? And if it does in fact shine, how much brighter could your beacon be? Every day, in every way, diligently strive to make your message one that is full of hope, light, and joy.

Be a lighthouse, not an outhouse.

Let your light shine before others,
so that they may see your good works
and give glory to your Father in heaven.
—MATTHEW 5:16 (NRSV)

Life is no brief candle to me.
It is a sort of splendid torch which I've got hold of
for the moment and I want to make it burn as brightly
as possible before handing it on to future generations.

—GEORGE BERNARD SHAW

Endeavor to live so that when you die,
even the undertaker will be sorry.

—MARK TWAIN

Be a good example.
If you can't be a good example
then you'll just have to be a horrible warning.

—CATHERINE AIRD

When You're Feeling Down, Do Like Duke

*S*orry all you rabid Blue Devils fans out there—I'm not talking about that highly esteemed university in North Carolina with a world-class basketball program. No, the reference here is to jazz-great Duke Ellington. He once said something that I believe is noteworthy in more ways than one (pun intended). When asked what motivated him to write so many incredible tunes, Duke replied, "I merely took the energy it takes to pout and wrote some blues." For the sake of the lesson set forth in these next few paragraphs, I think that quotation is worth repeating: "I merely took the energy it takes to pout and wrote some blues."

I don't know about you, but I know a lot of people out there who merely take the energy it takes to pout and use it to pout! If they're feeling down, they take the "woe is me" attitude towards life and are quick to let others know just how bad everything is. Positive thinking for these people comes to a virtual standstill when things don't go their way. And all too often they use the energy they do have to seek out other people or things that will make them feel even *more* down and out than they already are.

Here's a suggestion you might find helpful to keep in mind: The next time you're feeling bad, or upset, or bitter, or frustrated, take that negative energy and immediately use it to do something positive—something that makes you feel better physically, mentally and/or spiritually. Following are some examples from my own life: Since I like to exercise, I often will take about twenty minutes to do sets of push-ups if I feel discouraged or upset by something. Other times I'll go to the local driving range and hit away at a bucket of golf balls for thirty minutes or so. Still other times I simply sit down at my computer and write as if there were no tomorrow (in fact, the ideas for several of my books actually came about as a result of frantic writing to relieve frustration). And do you know what? I always, without fail, feel better and can think more clearly after doing any of these things.

What are a few constructive things that *you* really like to do? What are some positive activities you enjoy? The very next time you're down about something, don't give yourself the chance to wallow in your woe. Instead, as quickly as possible release your frustration, unhappiness, or anger by engaging in something positive; do something that will be a benefit to your body, mind and soul. If nothing else, your activity can be as simple as picking up the phone and calling someone you know who's a highly positive person and can help to cheer you up.

And you never know—your positive activity just might have positive effects on others, too. When Duke Ellington put his negative energy to positive use by writing blues, he not only helped himself; he brought happiness to millions of other people who fell in love with his music.

When you're feeling down, do like Duke!

A dead fish always floats downstream.
It takes a live fish to go against the current
and swim upstream.

—Source unknown

Silence is Golden,
so Make Your Words Platinum

*T*urn on any TV talk show and you'll find that most participants think they have something worthwhile to say...and yet, when you really listen to what is being said, they usually have nothing to say. Unfortunately, very little of what most people have to say is worth our time, and it is highly probable that very little of what you and I have to say is worth *their* time. It seems that we're all out there, more or less, just making a lot of noise!

A few years ago I came across an early American proverb

~ 28 ~

that said, "Don't speak unless you can improve the silence." I didn't give it much thought, and I turned the page to continue reading. Later in the day, however, the power of the quotation hit me because I remember going back to the book, finding the proverb, and reading it again: "Don't speak unless you can improve the silence." Wow! For someone like me who has always enjoyed talking, a saying like that can hit pretty close to home. The truth be told, however, this quotation has something important to say to all of us: Whoever we are, we should choose all our words carefully— very carefully.

I am fond of saying that people become wise by opening their ears, not their mouths (not that I always follow that advice to the letter, try as I might). By listening and gathering information, one is far better prepared to speak thoughtfully and intelligently when the time in fact *is* right to speak up. Yet most of us would much rather speak than be spoken to, apparently thinking that what we have to say is well worth everyone else's lending us an attentive ear.

Now please don't misunderstand what I am saying here; I do not mean to imply that one should not engage in light-hearted banter every now and then, or that words spoken in casual conversations around the coffee table must be carefully thought out all the time. (As the author of several books that blatantly encourage conversation, I am 100% for light, spontaneous chats.) More importantly, I want to be clear that I am *not* saying that one should be content to not say a word while others comment on important discussions or issues. Quite to the contrary, I am saying that by waiting to speak until you understand the implications of your words and the effects those words will have on your listeners, and by waiting to open your mouth until you have something truly valuable to say, you will be amazed at the positive impact your words can have. Abigail Van Buren could not have hit the mark more accurately when she declared, "The less you talk, the more you're listened to."

Which brings me to the simple fact that each of us must determine for ourselves what is really worth saying and what isn't, and each of us must recognize that we do indeed say plenty that is worth nobody's ear. The next time you are about to speak up—whether in your home, at the office, at a party, or anywhere else—you should consider asking yourself these four questions:

- Is what I am about to say constructive?
- Will my words put forth my point of view and still not put the listener/s on the defensive?
- Do my words provide the listener/s with helpful information?
- Do my words move the discussion along in a positive direction?

If you can't answer 'yes' to one or more of these questions, perhaps you should think some more before you speak. Above all else, whenever you are about to talk, be sure that what you intend to say is truly better than saying nothing at all.

Silence is golden, so make your words platinum.

It is better to be silent and be considered a fool than to speak and remove all doubt.

—Abraham Lincoln

If you keep your mouth shut, you won't put your foot in it.

—Source unknown

Silence at the proper season is wisdom,
and better than any speech.

—Plutarch

Silence is the voice of the convinced;
loudness is the voice of those
who want to convince themselves.

—Dagobert Runes

Speak when you are angry and you will make
the best speech you will ever regret.

—Ambrose Bierce

Wisdom is made up of ten parts,
nine of which are silence—the tenth, brevity.

—Source unknown

Climb Up, but Reach Down

*L*et's face it—the vast majority of us desire to see the view from the top of the mountain, whether it's in our personal life, professional life, or both. And in order to get to the top of Mount Success, each of us must climb a ladder (or rope!) of some sort or another.

Generally speaking, there are two obvious types of ladder-climbers: Those who rush toward the top while keeping their eyes firmly fixed on the final rung, and those who get to the first or second rung and decide that's about as far as they can go. I would suggest that neither of these ways brings any real happiness to the climber. One way is completely self-centered, while the other is absolutely self-defeating. If you want to find true joy on your ascent up the ladder of success, allow yourself to be a third type of ladder-climber—one who strives to climb high but constantly reaches down a hand to pull others up with him.

The fact is, as you reach down and encourage others to grow and succeed along with you, they in turn will eventually be able to help you in ways they couldn't before you helped *them.* And soon there will be two people who are moving upward, allowing greater synergy and potential in all future endeavors. Furthermore, as the people you have helped realize the difference you made in their life or career, they are likely to become a "teacher," or mentor, or encourager to someone else who needs an extended hand...and in this way, the links in the chain of success continue to grow and get stronger.

What about respect? Ultimate respect from other people

comes not because you've accomplished something great in and of itself, but because you've been a positive influence or role model for others. To see the truth of this, you probably need not look any further than your own circle of family or friends. I use as an example my own late grandfather, Dr. Herbert Nicholaus, a college professor for nearly 40 years. To this day, former students of his tell me of the deep respect they had for him; several have gone so far as to say that he was among the best role models they have had in their lives. None of them ever mentions the degrees that he earned; nobody mentions all the economics books to which he contributed; not one student has told me how impressed they were with all of his work and research in the field of accounting. No, the reason they admire him so much is because he cared deeply for each and every student and reached out to them on a regular basis. He would willingly spend hours one-on-one with someone who was struggling with the lessons. His home was *always* open to them, whether it was to discuss classroom work or life in general. From what my grandma told me many times, he never handed out one 'F' in all his years of teaching; he believed that if a student was putting forth an effort, he or she didn't deserve to fail the course, even if test scores indicated something to the contrary. As he was extending a helping hand to his students and in the process being a positive influence in their lives, he was gaining their life-lasting respect (whether he realized it or not).

Ultimately—and perhaps most gratifying—as you help others get ahead in life, you will experience a joy that can come only from giving of yourself. This kind of joy cannot be explained adequately, it must simply be experienced. By contrast, getting to the top of the ladder and realizing you are there all by yourself can leave you quite unsatisfied and very lonely indeed.

Climb up, but reach down.

There are two kinds of people on earth today,
Just two kinds of people, no more, I say.
Not the good and the bad, for 'tis well understood
That the good are half-bad and the bad are half-good.
No, the two kinds of people on earth I mean
Are the people who lift and the people who lean.

—ELLA WHEELER WILCOX

Be kind to the people you meet on the way up,
'cause you're going to meet the same people
on the way down!

—JACKIE GLEASON'S CHARACTER, RALPH KRAMDEN, ON *THE HONEYMOONERS*

A life is not important except in the impact
it has on other lives.

—JACKIE ROBINSON

Make Yourself Rich by Making Your Wants Few

Consider, if you will, the flip side of the statement listed above: The more you want, the poorer you will feel. Think about that for just a moment. Let's say you want a bigger house, a more luxurious car, a vacation to the islands, a larger investment portfolio, a summer cabin at the lake, season tickets to your favorite sports team, a membership to the local country club, a 48" TV with DVD player...the list goes on and on. When you consider all the things you want that you don't currently have, you will likely feel "poor." Compared to most people, you might actually be pretty well off, but it will always seem like you are running behind the Joneses as long as you continue to want what you don't have.

Now back to the original statement (which has actually been adapted slightly from a quotation by Henry David Thoreau). There are many reasons why you will indeed feel rich when you make your wants few, three of which I have listed here. For starters, because you don't desire or expect more and more all the time, everything you *do* get or have will genuinely excite you. I once heard a sales rep say about his commissions, "Five years ago, I was really motivated by the chance to make $50.00 on a sale, but not anymore; now it takes $500.00 to get me excited." What a shame that the commission that was once a thrill and a joy for this individual now almost seems like a burden to him. How high will the commission have to be to motivate this individual in five *more* years?!

Secondly, when you make your wants few, you eliminate a whole lot of stress and worry from your life because you don't feel the need to always reach the next level. We all know people loaded with money and other assets who say they are barely making it and need to work harder than ever to make ends meet. The reality is that their lifestyle continues to grow as their income does, so they continually need to make more and more money to pay off the things they have bought or to pay for those things they have become accustomed to doing and now believe they cannot live without. It's a never-ending, upward-moving, stress-inducing cycle.

Finally, by making your wants few, you will learn to appreciate and be deeply enriched by the simple elements life has to offer, much as Thoreau learned in the 1840s during his famous retreat at Walden Pond near Concord, Massachusetts. Things like the tranquil sound of a babbling brook in a pine-scented forest, multi-colored sunsets on the horizon, cooling breezes experienced from a porch swing on a warm summer night, or a relaxing walk along a moonlit shoreline just might make you feel like you are already rich in ways you wouldn't have even imagined before.

No quantity of material things will ever make you truly happy, no matter how much you acquire. You will always want more than you have, and that will lead to discontentment. But just a little of that which money cannot buy, if appreciated and embraced, will give you joy beyond belief. Perhaps Anne Morrow Lindbergh best summarized this entire concept of "less is truly more" when she said, "One cannot possibly collect all the beautiful shells on the beach. One can collect only a few, and they are more beautiful if they are few."

Make yourself rich by making your wants few.

If you want to know how rich you really are,
find out what would be left of you tomorrow
if you should lose every dollar you own tonight.

—W. J. BOETCKER

To be content with what we possess
is the greatest and most secure of riches.

—CICERO

The best things in life aren't things.

—ANN LANDERS

A poor person who is unhappy is in a better position
than a rich person who is unhappy. Why? Because the
poor person has hope: He thinks money would help!

—JEAN KERR

Accept Your Limitations and You'll Expand Your Potential

*E*arly on in his career, with things looking pretty bleak financially, he received a letter from a distributor in New York. Among other things, the letter forthrightly stated, "Everyone around here agrees your ideas are brilliant, but your execution clearly lacks something." The recipient of this letter had long been aware of the fact that he possessed great storytelling skills and filmmaking talents, but that his drawing abilities were definitely limited. So what did he do? He immediately set out to hire a gentleman by the name of Ub Iwerks, who became chief artist of the fledgling company. Over the next few years he hired some other men to work with Iwerks, among them Ward Kimball, Marc Davis, Ollie Johnston and Frank Thomas. He now had an entire team of highly qualified animators working for him, doing those things (such as animation) that he was not highly qualified to do himself. And animate they did...to the extent that *Snow White,* released in 1937, became what many consider to be one of the most successful movies of all time.

By now, you have no doubt figured out that the person I am writing about is Walt Disney—the man who built an entertainment empire and whose name is among the most recognizable brands in the world. But if you study Walt's story closely (something that I have enjoyed doing immensely over the last couple of years), you have to wonder how much—if any—of his success would have come about had he not recognized his own limitations and allowed others to do what he could not do well (for example, he turned over all financial planning to his brother and equal partner, Roy). After *Snow White*, Walt continued to focus on his strength—storytelling—while allowing his team to do the actual animation for such big-screen hits as *Bambi*, *Cinderella*, *Sleeping Beauty*, and *101 Dalmatians*, to name just a few. (Except for the initial concept sketch which he drew on the back of an envelope, even Mickey Mouse was usually drawn or animated by someone other than Walt.) Fortunately for those of us who love Walt Disney's movies—and everything else attributed to him—Walt took to heart the letter he received from that New York distributor. He put his own ego aside and realized that he could not significantly advance in his career until he accepted his own limitations.

I truly believe that one of the biggest stumbling blocks to success is a person's unwillingness to accept his or her own limitations; to put it very bluntly, one's ego gets squarely in the way and blocks large amounts of potential. We somehow think we are smart enough to learn it all and do it all ourselves...and as a result, we often go nowhere fast. NBA coach Phil Jackson said in his book *Sacred Hoops*, "The acceptance of boundaries and limits is the gateway to freedom." (Jackson writes that it wasn't until Michael Jordan truly understood this philosophy that he won the first of six NBA Championship rings.) Former UCLA coach John Wooden was fond of saying, "Do not let what you *cannot* do interfere with what you *can* do." As long-time coaches of extremely successful basketball teams, these two men understood something that many of us don't: When each individual focuses on the unique gift he or she possesses, while at the same time surrendering to the idea that other people's talents are required in order to win, winning in fact happens.

The famous pharmacy-chain founder Charles Walgreen

once said, "The most important thing I know is to surround myself with people who are smarter than I am." Given the incredible success of his company, it would be very difficult to argue against Walgreen's logic, which was really just his own way of saying, "I accept my limitations."

When we finally put our egos aside and admit that we cannot possibly do it all alone—that other people have abilities and talents which we do not possess but which we need to succeed—doing so mentally and physically frees us to focus and improve even more on what we *are* good at. When everyone concentrates on what he or she does best and uses those talents to help the "team," the results are often extraordinary.

Accept your limitations
and you'll expand your potential.

Their Interests, Shared Interests, Your Interests—in That Order

It never ceases to amaze me how much people love to talk about themselves. "Me, me, wonderful me! I've been there, I'm going here, I'm working on this, I've accomplished that, I believe this, I believe that...." In many people's minds, the starting point for most conversations has to be themselves. Attend any given party, business engagement, church get-together, or casual evening out with a few friends and see how quickly people begin to revolve the conversation around themselves. Trust me—you won't have to wait long!

Consider the following example: A woman is sitting at a lunch table with several friends and makes a comment such as, "We just got back from spending a week in sunny Florida"; in a split second, another person seated at the table issues the comment, "We usually go to Florida too, but we decided to go all out this year and do a seven-day cruise that took us to four tropical islands; it was the best vacation we've ever taken." The focus is immediately shifted to the person who took the "glorious" cruise and taken away from the person who went "only" to Florida.

Oddly enough, talking about oneself doesn't always occur in the positive sense, about good things that have happened; in fact, it is just as likely to happen with regard to bad things. A few years ago, I came across a quotation which aptly summarizes this idea. Dr. Andrew V. Mason, MD, wrote, "Sainthood emerges when you can listen to someone else's tale of woe and not respond with a description of your own." How many times have you or I heard someone say something like, "My dad has been recovering from a heart attack he had two months ago," only for someone else (or ourselves) to respond in the next breath with something like, "Well, just be thankful he's alive; my dad had a stroke two years ago and never recovered from it." Focus diverted. In another conversation, someone states, "My boss is really becoming difficult to work for." The person next to her responds with, "If you think your boss is difficult, you should work for *my* boss...." Focus again diverted. In both cases, the second person is implying that what he or she has to say is far more important than what the first person speaking has to say.

When I was a young child, my mom and dad would often tell me how important it is to let others have the stage. Since I was a very active, outgoing kid who enjoyed being in front of and having an audience, I had to work hard at that. As I went through school and got older, I tried to be extremely conscious about letting others have their moment. To this day, I take that concept very seriously; you should try and do the same. In no facet of daily life is this more important than with regard to the conversations you have—especially when others initiate the conversation or topic of discussion. As hard as it might be to accept, the cold, hard truth is this: People don't care about what *you* have to say until they know that you care about what *they* have to say. Period.

Harry Beckwith, founder of Beckwith Advertising and Marketing, and a past winner of the American Marketing Association's Effie, addresses this very issue in his book *Selling the Invisible*. According to Beckwith, the main reason businesspeople fail in their sales pitches is that they don't talk about the customer or what the customer wants, they instead talk about themselves and the products they are selling. With regard to the average Joe Salesperson, Beckwith tells the reader, "His pitch was all about him and what he had to sell, not about you and what you need. It was all about him. But what you cared about was you." He strongly encourages businesspeople to put the focus squarely on the needs of the customer and what the customer wants. He tells salespeople to forget talking about themselves or their products until they have first listened carefully and probed into what their customer needs. To put it bluntly, stop talking about yourself and start talking about them!

Whether in business, social, or even family situations, each of us must learn to put others' interests first. After a period of listening to them and demonstrating that you truly care about what they have to say, you can then talk about interests that the two of you share—common ground as it were. Finding common ground is the next step toward a healthy dialogue as it allows two people to discuss something that they both have a passion for or a knowledge of. Metaphorically speaking, establishing common ground allows you to "team up" with the other person and move forward as one. Lastly, and I do mean *lastly*, you can talk about *your* interests. By putting your own interests last, people will now be willing to listen to you and care about what you have to tell them. You'll be at the point where the other person can truly appreciate what you have to offer the discussion.

So the next time you strike up a conversation with someone else, remember that people need to know up front that you care about what they have to say. Let them have the stage. Avoid trying to "one-up" someone else's story. Show them non-verbally and verbally that their words really matter to you. Encourage them to tell you more by asking them questions that probe deeper into their concerns or thoughts about something. Rest assured, pretty soon they will start inquiring about *you*—and then you, too, will have some time in the limelight.

Their interests, shared interests, your interests—
in that order.

Half an hour's listening is essential except when
you are very busy. Then a full hour is needed.

—St. Francis de Sales

Listen—or thy tongue will keep thee deaf.

—American-Indian Proverb

The purpose of life is to listen—
to yourself, to your neighbor, to your world
and to God and, when the time comes,
to respond in as helpful a way as you can find.

—Fred Rogers ("Mister Rogers")

*The greatest gift you can give
another person is the purity
of your attention.*

—Richard Moss

*You can make more friends in two months
by becoming interested in other people
than you can in two years
by trying to get other people
interested in you.*

—Dale Carnegie

The Happiness of Your Life Depends Upon the Quality of Your Thoughts

—Marcus Aurelius

$\mathcal{T}$he Roman emperor and Stoic philosopher Marcus Aurelius understood a basic truth in the second century that has not changed a single bit in over 1,800 years: To improve your happiness, you must improve your thoughts.

Few among us have the ability to shatter an Olympic record; only a very small number of us have the talent to play the piano in a concert at Carnegie Hall; only a handful of us have the ability to perform life-saving, open-heart surgery.

But we are all equal in one area: Everybody—yes, everybody—has the ability to change or improve their thoughts and thus raise their level of happiness. Our 16th president, Abraham Lincoln, said, "Most folks are just about as happy as they make up their minds to be." It almost seems too elementary a statement to have any real merit, but Lincoln's plain-spoken wit hits the bullseye: The first step toward being happy is simply to think to yourself, "I'm happy, and life is good."

I know people (as I'm sure you do, too) who love telling me how terrible their life is, that the world is a bad place, and that there is very little good to be found anywhere anymore. These people are trapped in a permanent mode of negative thinking which blinds them from seeing all the good and wonderful things out there, even when those things are right in front of them. I feel sorry that these people will never see the beauty of their own lives or of the world around them.

About 10 years ago, there was a very popular country song entitled "Thinkin' Problem," and the first line of every refrain began with the words, "I've got a thinkin' problem...." (Obviously, this was a songwriter's clever play on a well-known phrase that relates to routinely imbibing too much alcohol.) Unfortunately, all of us are guilty to a greater or lesser degree of having a thinking problem—that is, too often we think the wrong kind of thoughts. We think along the lines of "Life is pretty unfair" when we should be thinking "Life is pretty good." We think "Things will never get better" when we should be thinking "Things will get better soon." We think "I can't" when we should be thinking "I can." Henry Ford once quipped, "Whether you think you *can* or you think you *can't*, you're right!"

Your life can be as full and meaningful as your thoughts allow, or as empty and meaningless as your thoughts allow. Your thoughts can lead you to do constructive things, or they can turn you in the direction of destructive actions. With that in mind, consider what Frank Outlaw has to say in these lines:

> **Watch your thoughts; they become words.**
> **Watch your words; they become actions.**
> **Watch your actions; they become habits.**
> **Watch your habits; they become character.**
> **Watch your character; it becomes your destiny.**

Pretty sobering, wouldn't you say? And in my opinion, absolutely true. What you are willing to *think* eventually determines the very core of who you are and what your destiny will be. Your mind is your window to happiness; if you don't keep it clean and bright, you will, over time, become increasingly unhappy, unpleasant, and negative. Virtually everything—whether good or bad—begins as a thought in your mind, eventually becoming something far greater or far worse down the line.

It's true that there is no way to control the thoughts of other people, but you can fully control your own. Every day, remind yourself to be determined to improve the quality of your thinking. You might even try to take 10 minutes a day to sit in a quiet place, close your eyes, and do absolutely nothing except think about positive, uplifting things. Do whatever works for you—so long as you are consciously striving to improve the quality of your thoughts; as a result, you'll see how your level of happiness in life goes up.

The happiness of your life depends upon
the quality of your thoughts.

*Nothing erases unpleasant thoughts more effectively
than conscious concentration on pleasant ones.*

—HANS SELYE

*Negative thinking can blind you to the good that
is out there, but you will never ruin your eyesight
by looking on the bright side of things.*

—SOURCE UNKNOWN

*The direction of your mind is more
important than its progress.*

—JOSEPH JOUBERT

In All Things, Humility

*I*t was around noontime on April 9th, 1865, when a Confederate soldier crossed the Union lines under a white flag. He carried with him a letter from General Robert E. Lee that was to be delivered to General Ulysses S. Grant. After four years of the most bloody warfare America has known to this day, and after well over 600,000 men had died in the American Civil War (more than 2% of the nation's population!), General Grant was about to receive a letter of surrender from General Lee. Grant opened the letter, looked at it, and then handed it to a friend to read aloud. The letter clearly stated that the South was surrendering and the war was over. One might fully expect that Grant, upon receiving this news, cheered out loud, that he threw his fists into the air in victory, that he celebrated like never before. Quite to the contrary, an eyewitness wrote in his journal, "Grant said not a thing [upon reading the letter]. He betrayed no more emotion than last year's birdnest." Years later, Grant himself would write about that moment, "I felt like anything rather than rejoicing at the downfall of a foe who had fought so long and valiantly."

During the surrender itself (which took place in the front parlor of a local citizen's house), Grant did everything possible to avoid showing even the slightest bit of arrogance or pride in his victory...to the point that he did not want to even *talk* about the South's surrender. Finally, historians have noted, Lee himself had to bring Grant back to the reason for their meeting: for Lee to surrender and effectively be taken as Grant's prisoner. The extremely generous terms offered by the North's general were signed by Lee (Grant even went so far as to offer 25,000 rations to the practically starving Confederate Army). Finally, the two men shook hands and departed. As Grant began to walk down the front steps of the McLean house, loud cheers rose up from the Union soldiers lined outside of the building; victory was theirs, after all, and they felt like celebrating. Grant immediately ordered the cheering to stop, and yelled out to his men, "We do not want to exalt over their [the Confederates'] downfall. The war is over; the Rebels are our countrymen again."

I am, to be sure, a Civil War buff, and would think this story a great one even if it did not have a poignant lesson to teach us; but it absolutely does, and so I have included it as a part of this chapter. If ever there were a good example of humility in the face of hard-earned victory, this is it. Grant had every reason to be filled with pride, to celebrate, to show-up his counterpart; he chose instead to do the exact opposite, and demonstrated that even in our proudest and most deserving moments, an air of humbleness can—and should—surround us.

The flip side of the coin, of course, shows a very different (and unfortunately, far more common) story. We routinely watch professional football figures celebrating like maniacs after a simple touchdown has been scored against their opponents; we witness corporate managers who walk all over their subordinates simply because their high position allows them to; we see movie stars who are quick to let us know by what they say, do and wear that they have "made it." Closer to home, there are neighbors who can't wait to tell you about their latest promotion at work, family members who are always talking about the great financial investments they've made, and friends who always want you to know how much they know.

And what about us? Surely we want everyone to know

what *we've* done, where *we're* heading, and how well *we're* doing in this or that. Certainly we want others to take notice of and praise our new car, our large house, our great job, our smart kids—and we stop at very little to make sure they do in fact recognize these things. Indeed, humility seems to be absent in many facets of our own lives.

Yet, in spite of all this, one of the greatest attributes we can nurture in our lives is humility. Throughout history, people have understood in their own day the importance of staying humble. Nearly 500 years ago, the leader of the Protestant Reformation, Martin Luther, said, "God created the world out of nothing, and as long as we are nothing, He can make something out of us." More than 200 years later, American theologian Jonathan Edwards stated, "Nothing sets a person so far out of the devil's reach as humility." In the nineteenth century, English reformer and writer John Ruskin wrote, "When a man is wrapped up in himself, he makes a very small package indeed." In more recent times, and speaking as a celebrity who had millions of adoring fans, Elvis Presley pronounced, "If your head gets too big, it will break your neck." (Although we may read this last quote with some sense of irony, the lesson it offers is by no means diminished.)

The problem of pride—or the lack of humility—has been around a long, long time. Due to the culture in which we live today, it may be harder than ever to practice humility, yet practice it we must. Do you want people to enjoy your presence? Learn to be humble. Do you want others to truly respect you? Practice humility in all things. If we were completely honest with ourselves, we would see no other way to live than humbly—for each of us is nothing more than a grain of sand on the ever-widening shore of human history. Ernest Legouve appropriately wrote, "If he could only see how small a vacancy his death would leave, the proud man would think much less of the place he occupies in his life-time."

Abraham Lincoln, who many would say is one of the most important figures in the history of our nation (or even the world), once said of himself, "I was born, and have ever remained, in the most humble walks of life." Quite frankly, I would argue that one of the reasons Lincoln has become such a beloved and highly respected figure is because of the very fact that he did not appear to recognize or call any attention to his own greatness. Even if only subconsciously, we very much respect humbleness such as that. We would do well to follow Lincoln's lead. Humble in our victories. Humble in our accomplishments. Humble in our speech. Humble in all things.

Perhaps the best way to close a chapter on humility is to quote from the Bible, a book that has a great deal to say about the importance of being humble. This particular quotation is taken from one of Christ's parables, recorded in Luke, chapter 14, verse 11. It says, quite simply, "For everyone who makes himself great will be humbled, and everyone who humbles himself will be made great."

In all things, humility.

The best way to be right
or wrong is humbly.

—SOURCE UNKNOWN

...What does the Lord require of you
but to do justice, and to love kindness,
and to walk humbly with your God.

—MICAH 6:8 (NRSV)

One Person with Passion is Better Than Forty Who Are Merely Interested

—TOM CONNELLAN

*T*om Connellan, author of the best-selling *Knock Your Socks Off* series, decided a few years ago to write a book detailing why the Walt Disney Company has been so successful through the years, with specific attention given to the success of Walt Disney World in Orlando, Florida. I suppose there are two main reasons why I chose to read his book *Inside the Magic Kingdom*: One, I am a huge fan of Walt Disney World, having made my first of roughly a dozen trips there when I was just three years old. Secondly, and more importantly, throughout the book Connellan describes in detail the importance of passion within the Disney culture—an attribute that I have long believed is underestimated and absolutely essential for success in any person's professional and personal life.

Allow me to give you a few quick examples of passion in business as I have witnessed them. The first example actually comes straight from one of my own trips to Walt Disney World, and it confirms what Connellan discovered first-hand while conducting research for the book. About five years ago, my family and I were waiting to catch a bus at our Disney resort, when a cast member (Disney's term for all of its employees) walked over and started talking with us. He was smiling and enthusiastic, giving us tips to make our vacation more enjoyable and providing us with some interesting background on the company. I asked him what he did, assuming he was probably involved in public relations or guest relations of some kind. Was I ever wrong! This man's sole job was to daily re-stock the small refrigerators in hundreds of hotel rooms on the property. Even more amazing than that was the fact that he had been doing this for several years and told us that he looked forward to doing it in the future.

Here was an individual who had a true passion for what he did, and someone who could serve as a model for us all. As our trip continued, I realized that virtually all the cast members seemed to share a similar passion for their work: the bus drivers, the ice-cream stand workers, the ride operators, the restaurant servers.... There is no doubt that their passion for what they do at Walt Disney World rubs off on the guests; it most certainly rubbed off on me. Their enthusiasm had a very positive impact on our entire vacation and greatly enhanced my family's already positive feelings for the place as a whole.

Example two: A guy in a small Midwest town who owns a popcorn shop. This gentleman sells more than 80 different flavors of popcorn, and his shop is always busy. Let me tell you why. Plain and simple, the owner has a passion for selling his product—popcorn! As soon as you walk in the door, he and his employees are greeting you and offering you free samples of warm, homemade popcorn. Soon he's asking you what else you'd like to try and how your day is going. He moves as fast and efficiently behind the counter as anyone I've seen, and his team of employees keeps pace with him. He absolutely loves his job and it shows. It makes people like me want to go into his shop and buy his product. His enthusiasm also makes him stand out from the dozens of other shops and eateries in the immediate area. Finally, I should note that his passion for what he does extends all the way to the popcorn recipes themselves; it is by far the best-tasting popcorn I have ever had anywhere!

Example three: An upscale gift shop in a quaint suburb of Chicago. The owner had heard about one of the Christmas books my publishing partner and I had published and decided that she wanted to sell the book in her store. She was passionate about the story. She read the short story to her employees, and they got excited about selling it. So excited about it that they began to hand-sell it to customers in the store. One December afternoon, the owner even read the story out loud so patrons in the store at the time could hear it. The end result? In just three weeks, this tiny shop had sold 75 copies of our book *The Christmas Letters*. Another gift store down the road had the same holiday title available; they were interested in selling it, but they were not *passionate* about selling it. Their final sales figures? They sold 6 copies during the same time period.

From Fortune 100 companies to mom-and-pop stores, from selling an entire corporate mindset to selling a specific product, I believe that nothing will help you succeed more than being passionate about what you do. Ralph Waldo Emerson once wrote, "Nothing great was ever achieved without enthusiasm." The greatest CEOs, generals, political and religious leaders, sports figures, inventors, educators, and earth-shakers of every kind and every generation all prove Emerson's quotation to be true. It has also been said that nothing is as contagious as enthusiasm. Enthusiastic attitudes rub off on others, and those people then use their new-found passion to get even more people excited—and in this way the cycle of enthusiasm continues to grow and gather steam.

As much as you can, try to surround yourself with passionate people, and keep in mind that a small number of passionate individuals will almost always achieve far more than a much larger group of "just interested" ones. When it comes to your own work, do you count yourself as one of those passionate people? If not, you should carefully consider what your options are for increasing your enthusiasm level. However, you shouldn't think of passion only as it relates to your work or career. In fact, in many ways, passion is even more important in other areas of life. I believe that passion for your faith, passion for your marriage, and passion for your kids are three of the most important. Just imagine what life would be like if everyone were more passionate in these three areas!

Finally, keep in mind that a wonderful byproduct of true passion is perseverance. Passion, in fact, is what allows you to persevere when the going gets tough—and we all know that the going *will* get tough sooner or later. (Remember Passion and Perseverance as the "Two Ps for Success.") Being interested can get you out of the starting blocks, but you will need passion to keep you continuously moving toward the finish line.

One person with passion is better than forty who are merely interested.

The gap between enthusiasm and indifference is filled with failures.

—Source unknown

Success is going from failure to failure without losing your enthusiasm.

—Abraham Lincoln

Knowledge is power, but enthusiasm pulls the switch.

—Ivern ball

Remember Jack and Ben

$\mathcal{A}$s an avid golfer, I have always been intrigued by the "thinking" side of this game called golf. It seems to me that perhaps more than any other sport, golf requires mental acumen in order for a person to be truly successful. Because of this fact, I really enjoy hearing what professional golfers on the various Tours have to say about how they prepare mentally for tournaments. As I have listened to their words over many years, I have discovered that what these professionals have to say about golf often can be put to use in day-to-day living.

There are two golfing statements that I remember better

than any others, and I feel that both of them have significant value for our lives *off* the course. The first statement—actually a theory, I suppose—is by the winner of the most professional Majors in golf history, Jack Nicklaus (he won 18 of them). One Sunday afternoon, I was listening to a golf commentator on TV talk about how professionals handle the pressure of leading a tournament as they go into the final round on Sunday, specifically with regard to what they do when they start the final round with a couple of bad holes. The announcer brought up a story of how Jack Nicklaus once said that he handled poor starts to final rounds in tournaments. Jack said that he always figured that every golfer playing the golf course on that given day was going to have his fair share of bad holes. Virtually nobody gets through a round unscathed, he said, so it's just a matter of time before your bad hole—or holes—pop up. Jack concluded his theory by saying that he never got bent out of shape or even concerned if he started his round with a bogey or two. If his bad holes came early on, he would surely have good holes to offset those as the round progressed. On the other hand, he thought, those golfers starting out really well would eventually be bogeying some holes (while, presumably, Nicklaus was busy sinking birdie putts). The commentator relaying the story admitted that he thought this was one of the best golfing philosophies he had ever heard.

A second but somewhat similar story comes from another beloved golfer who also won his share of professional Majors (including three out of four in 1953), Ben Hogan. Hogan once said that in a typical 18-hole round of golf, he would usually hit only two or three shots exactly the way he had planned. Just two or three! Even if you eliminate putting strokes from the equation, that means that Ben hit only three shots out of 40 the way he thought he should—less than 8%; roughly 92% of his shots didn't come off the clubface the way he had envisioned or expected them to. And this from a man that many knowledgeable golf aficionados consider to have had the best swing in the history of the game!

Out in the real world, where there is a lot more at stake than racking up the birdies and winning a golf tournament, we might do well to take to heart what these two golf icons have said. First of all, you must understand that no matter how good you are in your work, your marriage, raising children, or just making headway in life, there are going to be setbacks along the way. You must from the outset accept the old adage that into every life some rain will fall. To be honest, the vast majority of the things you do—or that happen to you—in life may seem less than perfect or ideal, falling short of the mark you set. But you must also keep in mind that you will have your share of moments when all is right, when you know you've nailed it, when it doesn't get any better, when you wonder why it can't be this easy or enjoyable all the time. Your moments in the sun will surely arrive, but you must be willing to wait out the storms and commit yourself to staying the course.

Remember, too, that you are not alone. Everyone is going to have bad days, bad times, and unexpected situations that he or she will have to deal with. And for every person out there, good days and good times will also come. When you are having a bad day, a friend of yours may be having a great day; when times are happy for you, they may be very difficult for your friend. Good times and bad times seem to spread themselves out among everyone. Myrtle Reed understood this idea well when she said, "Somewhere on this great world the sun is always shining, and it will sometimes shine on you."

Yes, some dark clouds are sure to pass your way; but bright, magnificent days will be yours to embrace as well. Whether in your career, with your family, or in your personal development, accept the bad...and with open arms be prepared to greet the good that is yet to come.

Remember Jack and Ben.

If all our misfortunes were laid in one common heap
whence everyone must take an equal portion,
most people would be contented
to take their own and depart.

—SOCRATES

A certain amount of opposition is a great help to
a person. Kites rise against, not with the wind.

—JOHN NEAL

Be Caring and Compassionate—Constantly

$\mathcal{O}$ne of my favorite stories that my mom tells goes back to the days when she had just started dating the man who would one day become my dad. They were eating at a corner restaurant in Chicago, talking about their enjoyable evening at the movies, when suddenly my dad excused himself from the table, rushed past the cash register, and went outside. My mom had no idea what was going on, until, a few seconds later, she looked out the window—only to see my dad helping a middle-aged blind man cross the busy street. Dad had apparently noticed the cane he was holding, and even though the blind man was undoubtedly used to crossing streets on his own, dad felt the need to go out and at least offer his help. I have always relished this story because it provides such a wonderful snapshot of who my dad was, day in and day out. He was thoughtful. He was caring. He was compassionate.

Because of the way I was raised, I remain to this day acutely aware of the compassion this world so desperately needs. On the other hand, as you might expect, the vast majority of the people I know live in nice homes, make a decent living, have pretty solid families, and enjoy good health. It would be very easy for me to just sit back and put blinders on, content to let the world pass by; regrettably, I do at times make use of those blinders. But I try hard to keep my eyes open, looking for opportunities to say or do something to help someone else. Often, I don't even need to look beyond my own neighborhood or street. The opportunities to show someone I care are literally everywhere.

What about you? Are you sitting back when it comes to practicing compassion? If you are, get yourself up. Don't rest any longer. Don't turn away from those who are hurting. Stop kidding yourself by saying, "Oh, someone else will help them, I'm sure." Perhaps *you* are the one who is supposed to help them. Maybe that particular person or cause needs *your* compassion right now. Someday, *you* just might be in that same position, in need of someone else's help.

Take time to care in every area of life. Buy cookies from little kids who are selling them. Spend a half hour or so with an elderly person who would love nothing more than to have someone sit and listen to a few stories from yesteryear. Hold the door open for someone who has her arms full. When someone you know dies, take the time to write a personal note to the family, telling them how much the deceased person meant to you. Always say "Thank you" to veterans who have served our country. Give a tight hug to someone who needs it. Say things in a manner that lets other people know you care about their feelings. Offer your time and talents in a service project. Give money, as much as you can, to legitimate organizations that help those in need. Buy a sandwich and a bowl of soup for a homeless person. Give that same homeless person an old coat of yours that will keep him warm. Pray for those people and causes which are brought to your attention but that you cannot personally help. Ask God to give you a more caring and compassionate heart.

Make a conscious commitment to be more caring and compassionate toward others, if for no other reason than because it is the right thing to do. There is also an indescribable level of joy that comes from helping those less fortunate than you. With that in mind, we would all do well to ponder the words of Dr. Albert Schweitzer: "I don't know what your destiny will be, but one thing I know: the only ones among you who will be truly happy are those who have sought and found how to serve."

Be caring and compassionate—constantly.

It is one of the most beautiful compensations of this life that no man can sincerely try to help another without helping himself.

—RALPH WALDO EMERSON

To be blind is bad, but worse it is to have eyes and not to see.

—HELEN KELLER

Winning the Rat Race is the Ultimate Trap

A couple years back, a woman I was talking to told me that her mother's favorite expression was, "Even if you win the rat race, you're still a rat." As clever and humorous as this saying is, I certainly don't think it's wholly true. After all, I know quite a few people who are serious contenders in the rat race, but I definitely wouldn't classify them as rats! In fact, many of them are wonderful people who probably mean well in what they are doing, trying to get as far ahead as they can so that they can better provide for their families.

But therein lies the trap: As people work harder and harder to achieve or acquire more and more, something invariably has to give. In some cases, marriages go on the rocks or dissolve completely; in others, children with no at-home parents develop serious social or behavioral troubles; in yet others, major health problems surface as a result of the fast pace they choose to take. A friend of mine, who is much older than I am, had for years been working 70-hour weeks to get himself higher and higher up in the company he worked for. That was about a decade ago, before he suffered a massive stroke. He hasn't worked a single day since, and he still suffers from serious physical disabilities as a result of the incident.

In the pursuit of more money, more power, more prestige, more glory, more whatever, invariably time and energy become misdirected to a greater or lesser degree. Even those individuals among us who are busy for the noblest of reasons may well have regrets when it is all said and done. A few years back, the Rev. Billy Graham was interviewed by the late John F. Kennedy, Jr. for an article that appeared in his magazine, *George*. Toward the end of the interview, Dr. Graham was asked if he had any regrets in his life. His response? "Just one. I only wish I had spent more time with my family."

Every one of us lives in a fast-paced, high-stress world where it is incredibly easy to get caught up in the rat race of life. To some degree being in the race is unavoidable, but we must always be careful that we don't run too hard. Sadly, as was the case with my friend, you may not even know the race has trapped you until it is too late. If you win the rat race— or strive to win it—you won't necessarily be a rat...but I can assure you that someday you will be looking back with regrets of one form or another.

Winning the rat race is the ultimate trap.

*What you have become is the price you paid
to get what you used to want.*

—MIGNON MCLAUGHLIN

*A pint can't hold a quart—if it holds a pint than it is
doing all that can possibly be expected of it.*

—MARGARET DELAND

*One by one the sands are flowing,
One by one the moments fall;
some are coming, some are going...
do not strive to grasp them all.*

—ADELAIDE PROCTOR

Please, Say "Thank You"

 I often find myself in restaurant settings where there are a fair number of people seated with me at the table. Having frequent exposure to good-sized groups of people like that gives me a chance to regularly test the theory that people just don't know the importance of saying "Thank you" anymore. Not too long ago, I was seated with quite a few other people in a rather casual, full-service restaurant. When the gentleman came to the table to pour water for each of us, I was the only one who thanked him for his effort. When the waitress delivered the food to our table, the number of thankers got better—by one person (a colleague of mine and I). Yet when the waitress returned ten minutes later to see how the food was and if there was anything else we needed, I again was the only one who actually thanked her for asking. Sadly, I routinely find that I am among an extremely small number of people saying "Thank you" in situations where thank-yous are warranted. Now please don't misunderstand: I don't mention these things to suggest that I should receive this year's award for Mr. Manners; rather, I include the story above to make the point that most people out there seem to drastically underestimate the importance of gratitude—whether in a restaurant, at home, at work, or anywhere else.

In his national best-selling business book *How to Become CEO*, Jeffrey Fox dedicates an entire chapter to the importance of being polite to everyone with whom you come into contact. In yet another chapter, he lists—based on his experiences—what he considers to be the top 10 things you should say if you want to make people feel good. Number 1 on his list is "Please." What do you think Number 2 is? That's right—"Thank You." Fox writes, as one example, that a good manager should find a reason to say "Thank you" a minimum of 20 times a day. That's at least 100 times per week! Unfortunately, we all know from personal experience that most people—both in and out of managerial positions—fall far short of that total.

It is probably obvious to almost everyone reading this that saying nice things to people helps those people to feel good about themselves. What we often forget, however, is that when people are thanked and made to feel that what they did truly meant something, they end up contributing even more and working at a higher level than before. I personally know several people who, as a result of being thanked, will go out of their way to do even more the next time they're called upon for something. Now be careful with that: Thanking should never, ever be used in an exploitative way or as a mere formality; that's wrong, and a high percentage of people will see right through it. Instead, every "Thank you" should come from the heart with total sincerity. Higher productivity, deeper respect and better cooperation are simply great byproducts of kind words honestly spoken.

I don't care who you are or what you do, it is always gratifying to receive gratitude for something you've done—whether it's pouring a glass of water in a restaurant or saving the big account that everyone in the company thought was lost. Everybody wants to feel appreciated; it is, after all, one of our most basic desires as human beings. Simply saying "Thank you"—and meaning it—is one of the easiest and, as Jeffrey Fox concurs, best ways to make someone feel happy.

You might also consider other ways to thank people in your life, such as regularly writing thank-you notes on nice stationery, sending beautiful flowers, or taking someone out for a "Thank you" dinner (especially someone who's not expecting it). And one more thing: By all means, politely remind those around you of the importance of thanking people on a daily basis.

Please, say "Thank you."

Silent gratitude isn't much use to anyone.
—Gladys Browyn Stern

The hardest job kids face today is learning good manners without seeing any.
—Fred Astaire

It is possible for a man wholly to disappear and be merged in his manners.
—Henry David Thoreau

Accomplishments Are Seldom Bigger Than the Size of Your Dreams

What must one do in order to be successful in life? If you asked this question to any random group of people, it is likely that you would hear such answers as these: Prepare well, work hard at all times, persevere in tough times, maintain a high level of passion (see lesson #12), create your own "luck"...the list goes on. To be sure, each and every one of these things—and others—are essential if one is going to be successful in personal or professional life.

There is one ingredient, however, that quite often gets overlooked in the recipe for success; and in many ways it is the most important element. That element is what I refer to as the big dream. The big dream comes before anything else and allows you to imagine—or, more accurately, *believe*—the seemingly impossible, that thing which nobody else around you thinks can be accomplished.

The big dream, in fact, should be so big that it almost encourages other people to think that your head is in the clouds and that you need to wake up and get in touch with reality. The big dream should constantly inspire you, in both good times and bad times, to reach much higher than where you currently are, and certainly to reach higher than others think you can. In the midst of all the doubtful voices around you, you must never give up the belief that your big dream is achievable. The skeptics out there will tell you that dreams are for impractical people, for those who don't live in the "real world." Much to the contrary, I would argue that to be successful in the real world, your dreams have to be *out* of this world!

The best quote I have ever seen with regards to dreaming big is by Bob Moawad. He asserts the following: "How exciting are your dreams? Most people don't aim too high and miss—they aim too low and hit!" If you pause to think about it, that quotation serves to remind us all of the completely backward perspective most of us have when it comes to our dreams.

I am the first to admit that I am sometimes guilty of aiming lower than I should with regard to my own dreams. I am keenly aware of the level that I can comfortably achieve, and at times that is what I shoot for. Sure enough, I usually achieve it. For example, if I set a goal for myself to sell 10,000 copies of a given book I have written, that is usually in the ballpark of the number of books that I will actually sell; I will work just hard enough to get to that level of success. If I set a goal of 25,000 copies, sales are usually fairly close to the 25,000-copy figure. The point is that I know I could go much further if I allowed myself to dream bigger right from the start. Fortunately for me, my business partner loves to dream huge on every project, and with respect to the books on which we've collaborated, he has gotten us to higher levels of success than I would have ever arrived at on my own. (For example, with our very first book, *The Conversation Piece*, he set a sales goal so high that almost everyone else, including me, thought he was crazy. It eventually became a national bestseller and has been our best-selling book to date, while continuing to move ever closer to his original, lofty goal.) Remember: Your level of productivity, passion, and perseverance is determined largely by the size of your dream. By raising the bar on your dream, all else will be elevated accordingly.

Advertising agency executive Leo Burnett once said, "When you reach for the stars, you may not quite get one, but you won't come up with a handful of mud either." What about you? Are you reaching for the stars? On a "dream scale" of 1 to 10 (where 1 is "easily achievable" and 10 is "virtually out of reach"), are you generally content to get to level 2, 3, or 4? If so, that is about as far as you will go. But if you aim high and believe you can reach level 8, 9, or even 10, there is a decent chance that you in fact will. As Burnett's quotation reminds us, even if you shoot for 10 and never quite get there, you will get a lot closer than if you had from the beginning goaled yourself to reach a much lower level.

What dreams do you want to achieve with regard to your family, your work, or your life as a whole? Are you aiming high or low? Will you content yourself with mediocrity or will you settle only for the best? Will you fix your eyes on some distant pinnacle, or will you focus them on a much lower and closer plateau that you know you can reach with relative ease?

There will be a time for hard work, passion, perseverance, and all the other things that are needed for true success...but in the beginning you must first and foremost dream big and determine that you are going after that dream. Your outlandish dream precedes all else; everything else springs forth from it. Dream big dreams and reach for the stars—you just might get one!

Accomplishments are seldom bigger
than the size of your dreams.

Make no little plans;
they have no magic to stir men's blood.
—Daniel Burnham

*Aim for the top; there is plenty of room there.
There are so few at the top, it's almost lonely.*

—Samuel Insull

*Don't be afraid to go out on a limb—
that's where the fruit is found.*

—H. Jackson Brown

*Aerodynamically, the bumblebee shouldn't
be able to fly; but the bumblebee doesn't know it
so it goes on flying anyway.*

—Mary Kay Ash

*The poorest of all folks is not the person without a cent,
but the person without a dream.*

—Source unknown

There Are Always More Lessons to Learn

$\mathcal{L}$essons. They come from books, both old and new. They come from people, both young and old. They come from relationships. They come from speeches, sermons, and conversations with friends. They come from what we have done right and from what we have done wrong. They come in forms we don't expect and when we least expect them. They come during every stage of our lives, and they keep on coming.

There are always more lessons to learn...the question is

whether we are willing to be taught. It is so very easy for us to think that we know it all, that we have already learned every lesson in life that we need to learn. Regardless of how old you are, resist this way of thinking with everything inside you. There are *always* more lessons to learn.

Some lessons will have the power to radically change your life. Some will change the way you think about something or someone. Some lessons will make you laugh, while others may cause you to cry. Some lessons will be learned over the course of many years, whereas others will be learned in a matter of seconds. Keep your eyes and ears open for life's lessons; they are abundant. The person who routinely welcomes more of life's lessons and learns from them becomes wiser right along, and the way of wisdom leads to greater happiness.

Take a little time and write down some of the more important lessons you have learned in life. Furthermore, consider sharing them with your family and friends. Ask these people what lessons life has taught—or is now teaching—them. Learn from one another. Sharing our many diverse lessons with each other can be truly inspiring, enlightening, and a great deal of fun.

To be sure, there are many more lessons that could have become full essays in this book, but time and space permitted for just 18 to be written out in full-chapter format. I would, however, like to leave you with just a few more lessons, some parting thoughts if you will. There are no details or stories behind these lessons, just the lessons themselves. Perhaps you will find some of these to be as applicable to your life as the full-length lessons were.

There is no doubt in my mind that by the time this book finds its way into your hands, I will have experienced some new lessons that I will wish I had included in this collection. But if I waited to publish this book until I had experienced all that life has to teach me, the project, quite frankly, would never be released.

There are always more lessons to learn.

- **Stop praying for things and start praying for people.**

- **Be tough on yourself but go easy on others.**

- **Write out a mission statement for your life.**

- **Find a hero for yourself.**

- *Your reputation is your resumé.*
  —MADELEINE ALBRIGHT

- **Take a little time each day to do absolutely nothing.**

• Smiles, everyone, smiles!

• Each week, memorize one great quotation.

• *Sandwich every bit of criticism
between two layers of praise.*
—MARY KAY ASH

• Celebrate everything—not just the milestones,
but the little moments as well.

• *Human happiness and moral duty
are inseparably connected.*
—GEORGE WASHINGTON

About the Author

Bret Nicholaus is a full-time writer and speaker who has authored or co-authored 19 books, including the national best-selling *Conversation Piece* series and the popular, heartwarming holiday story *The Christmas Letters*. Altogether, more than 600,000 copies of his books have been sold. He holds a degree in speech communication from Bethel University, St. Paul, MN. Nicholaus is, in fact, a huge fan of lemonade—especially the pink variety with lots of pulp. He and his family live in the Chicago area.